THE GREAT BIG
PUMPKIN
COOKBOOK

A Quick and Easy Guide to Making Pancakes, Soups, Breads, Pastas, Cakes, Cookies, and More

Maggie Michalczyk, RDN

Skyhorse Publishing

10 9 8 7 6

Cover design by Kai Texel
Photography by Maggie Michalczyk and Megan Neveu

Library of Congress Control Number: 2020930857

Print ISBN: 978-1-5107-5919-0
eBook ISBN: 978-1-5107-5920-6

Printed in the United States of America

CONTENTS

BREADS, BITES & BARS . . . 41

COOKIES . . . 63

DIPS & PASTAS . . . 79

SOUPS & CHILIS . . . 93

ACKNOWLEDGMENTS

Sponsors of this book include Simple Mills, Libby's, Quaker, and siggi's dairy. I'm proud to partner with these amazing brands to bring you recipes highlighting their delicious and nutritious products.

Guest photography by Megan Neveu

INTRODUCTION

Why pumpkins?! People always ask me how my love affair with this fall vegetable (technically a fruit) started. My answer is simple. Pumpkins make people happy. They represent the nostalgia of the season, a time we look forward to all year long and love to celebrate.

I love the magic that I feel in the fall—the leaves changing colors, picking the perfect pumpkin, and baking something that makes your whole house smell delicious. It makes my soul happy!

Autumn inspires me to cook and bake with pumpkin in new ways—I love that you can do so much with it in both sweet and savory recipes and I can't wait for you to discover all of the possibilities in this book!

These recipes focus on simple, nutrient-dense ingredients. I always try to sweeten things naturally and add more nutrition whenever possible. Most of the recipes you will find in this book do just that, and some are classics that have been left untouched.

Pumpkin adds nutrition, texture, flavor, and flair to all of the recipes in this book that I hope will inspire your adventures in the kitchen and help you celebrate the season we all love!

For pumpkin recipes and more, be sure to follow me @onceuponapumpkin or visit onceuponapumpkinRD.com.

XOXO Maggie

NUTRITIONAL BENEFITS OF PUMPKIN

Packed with fiber

Good source of potassium

Great source of vitamin A

Good source of vitamin C

Great source of lutein and zeaxanthin—imperative for eye health

Bursting with antioxidants

Helps promote healthy skin

TYPES OF PUMPKINS

Did you know there are over one hundred types of pumpkins varieties?! Each year plant breeders evaluate and select from among thousands of new pumpkin lines to find the right combination of traits to make the best pumpkin possible. I love that every pumpkin is different and beautiful in its own way.

Fairytale

Gladiator

Cannon Ball

Rhea

Lil' Pump-Ke-Mon

Miniwarts

Little Giant

Crunchkin

Munchkin

These images are courtesy of HM.CLAUSE. For over 15 years HM.CLAUSE has been a leader in pumpkin breeding, and continues to bring unique and innovative varieties to market today.

25 WAYS TO USE A CAN OF PUMPKIN

The pumpkin possibilities are endless

1. **QUESADILLAS** Spread 2 tbsp. of pumpkin puree on tortillas and top with shredded cheddar cheese, chicken, sautéed spinach & black beans. Top with second tortilla and sauté on a pan until crispy and golden brown.

2. **DEVILED EGGS** Halve 12 hard-boiled eggs. Mash yolks with ½ cup pumpkin and plain Greek yogurt, 1 tsp. Dijon mustard, and ½ tsp. each salt and ground coriander. Spoon into egg whites.

3. **MUSTARD** Mix 2 tbsp. each pumpkin, grainy mustard, and honey.

4. **VINAIGRETTE** Whisk 2 tbsp. each apple cider vinegar and pumpkin and 1 tsp. Dijon mustard; whisk in ¼ cup extra-virgin olive oil. Add a pinch of salt, pepper, and red pepper flakes for a kick.

5. **CREAM CHEESE** Mix ½ cup pumpkin with 1 package ⅓ less fat cream cheese or dairy-free cream cheese. Add 2 tbsp. honey and 1 tbsp. pumpkin pie spice.

6. **YOGURT** Stir ¼ cup pumpkin puree and 1 tsp. pumpkin pie spice into the yogurt of your choice.

7. **SMOOTHIE** Add ¼ cup pumpkin to your favorite smoothie combination to thicken the texture and add more nutrition!

8. **OATMEAL** Simmer 1½ cups unsweetened almond milk with 1 cup old-fashioned oats, ½ cup pumpkin, 2 tsp. pumpkin pie spice, and a splash of vanilla extract until creamy. Top with sliced almonds, pecans, banana slices, berries, or a heaping tbsp. of nut butter.

9. **APPLESAUCE** Simmer 4 chopped and peeled apples, 1 cup water, ½ cup pumpkin, and ½ cup sugar or coconut sugar, the juice of one lemon, and a cinnamon stick. Stir occasionally, mashing with a fork, for 12 minutes.

10. **WAFFLES & PANCAKES** Add ⅓ cup pumpkin puree to your favorite waffle or pancake mix for an extra moist texture, fall flavor, and nutrition.

11. **PASTA SAUCE** Stir ¼ cup pumpkin into your favorite pasta sauce.

12. **CHILI** Add 1 can of pumpkin to your classic chili recipe and continue simmering until incorporated.

13. **CURRY** Mix 1 can of pumpkin into your favorite curry recipe for a thicker, more flavorful version.

14. **MEATBALLS** Mix ½ cup pumpkin into 1¼ lb. lean ground turkey plus ¼ cup almond flour, 1 large egg, 2 cloves garlic (minced), 2 tsp. Italian seasoning, 1 tsp. ground sage, 1 tsp. thyme, ½ tsp. crushed red pepper, and salt and pepper to taste. Roll into balls and bake on a cookie sheet at 425° F for 18–20 minutes.

15. **TAPENADE** In a food processor, combine 1 cup pumpkin with ½ cup kalamata olives, ⅓ cup sun-dried tomatoes (not packed in oil), 2 cloves of garlic, finely chopped, 1 tbsp. of basil, and ¼ cup extra-virgin olive oil. Pulse, and add salt and pepper to taste. Serve on top of crusty Italian bread or grilled chicken.

16. **"NICE" CREAM** Freeze 3 bananas (without the peels). Add frozen bananas to a high-speed blender with ½ cup pumpkin, 2 tsp. pumpkin pie spice, 1 tsp. vanilla, and a splash of almond milk. Blend to combine. Scoop into a loaf pan, refreeze for an hour, then scoop and enjoy.

17. **MILKSHAKE** Blend ½ cup pumpkin with ¼ cup milk of choice, ½ banana, and ¾ cup your favorite vanilla ice cream until smooth. Pour into a glass and top with pecans and pumpkin seeds or pumpkin granola.

18. **FUDGE** Mix ⅓ cup pumpkin with ¾ cup creamy peanut butter, ¼ cup melted coconut oil, 1 tbsp. maple syrup, and 2 tsp. pumpkin pie spice. Line a loaf pan with parchment paper and add the mixture to the pan, smoothing it out with a spatula. Freeze for 15 minutes, and then remove and cut into squares. Store in the freezer.

19. **HOT COCOA** Stir together 1 cup milk of your choice (I recommend almond milk or oat milk) with 2 tbsp. unsweetened cocoa powder, 1 tbsp. pumpkin puree, 1 tbsp. maple syrup, and a dash of pumpkin pie spice.

20. **ICE CUBES** Store leftover canned pumpkin in an ice cube tray and freeze. Pop cubes into future soups and smoothies!

21. **PALEO PUMPKIN MUG CAKE** Combine 2 tbsp. pumpkin, 2 tbsp. coconut flour or almond flour, 1 egg beaten, ¼ tsp. baking soda, 1 tsp. pumpkin pie spice, ½ tsp. vanilla, and a splash of maple syrup in a mug or small ramekin. Microwave for about a minute and a half and enjoy with fruit on top.

22. **POPSICLES** In a small bowl combine 1 cup pumpkin, 1 tbsp. maple syrup, and 1 tsp. pumpkin pie spice. In another small bowl, combine 1½ cups Greek yogurt, and ½ cup milk of choice. Layer the yogurt and pumpkin mixture in popsicle molds until they are full. Freeze for at least 6 hours.

23. **FACE MASK** Whisk together ¼ cup pumpkin, ¼ cup Greek yogurt, 2 tbsp. raw honey, and 1 tsp. cinnamon. Smooth a generous amount over your face and leave on for 15–20 minutes until almost dried before washing off. *Pumpkin is a great source of vitamin C, which helps brighten skin and boost collagen production.*

24. **SUGAR SCRUB** Combine ½ cup brown sugar, 2 tbsp. pumpkin, 2 tbsp. coconut oil, 2 tsp. pumpkin pie spice, and 1 tsp. vanilla extract. Rub onto dry skin and rinse off. *Pumpkin contains vitamin E, which helps to nourish and protect the skin.*

25. **FOR A DOG'S UPSET STOMACH** Soothe your pup's tummy troubles with the power of pumpkin! Give smaller dogs 1 tsp. of canned pumpkin, and larger dogs approximately 1 tbsp.

BASICS

HOMEMADE PUMPKIN PUREE

Roasting your own pumpkin at home to make pumpkin puree is easier than you think!

PREP TIME: 10 MIN. • COOKING TIME: 25 MIN.

INGREDIENTS

Makes 1 ½ cups
1 2–4-lb. pie or sugar
    pumpkin

DIRECTIONS

1. Preheat the oven to 415° F. Line a baking sheet with parchment paper and set aside.

2. Using a sharp knife, cut the top off of the pumpkin, scoop the seeds out, and clean out any of the remaining stringy insides.

3. Cut the pumpkin into 4 equal pieces.

4. Place flesh down on a baking sheet and bake for 25 minutes and let cool.

5. Once cooled, remove the skin using your hands or a paring knife.

6. Place the pumpkin flesh in a food processor and pulse for about 5 minutes until puree begins to form.

7. Store in a container in the fridge for up to a week or freeze.

HOMEMADE
PUMPKIN PIE SPICE

Photograph by Megan Neveu

Did you know pumpkin spice is actually made up of a blend of spices?! It's easy to make yourself at home and can be used in so many different ways!

PREP TIME: 5 MIN.

INGREDIENTS

Makes ¼ cup
3 tbsp. ground cinnamon
2 tsp. ground ginger
1 tsp. ground allspice
1½ tsp. ground nutmeg
½ tsp. ground cloves

DIRECTIONS

1. Mix all individual spices together in a small jar— sprinkle on everything all fall long!

HOMEMADE PUMPKIN SPICE OAT MILK LATTE

Skip the coffeehouse version, which is traditionally packed with extra sugar and calories, and make your own at home instead with real pumpkin! This pumpkin spice oat milk latte is creamy and spiced just right for the season.

PREP TIME: 5 MIN. ● GLUTEN & DAIRY FREE

INGREDIENTS

Makes 1 serving
8 oz. brewed coffee
2 tsp. pumpkin puree
3 tbsp. oat milk
Sprinkle of homemade
   pumpkin spice for
   topping

DIRECTIONS

1. Combine all ingredients except for the pumpkin spice in a Vitamix or high-speed blender. Blend until frothy.

2. Pour into coffee mug and top with homemade pumpkin spice and enjoy!

BREAKFAST

PUMPKIN SPICE ALMOND BUTTER

Smooth and creamy with a hint of pumpkin spice! Make pumpkin spice almond butter and put it on toast or pair with apple or banana slices.

PREP TIME: 10 MIN. • GLUTEN & DAIRY FREE

INGREDIENTS

Makes 1½ cups
2½ cups dry roasted, unsalted almonds
1 tbsp. pumpkin pie spice
1 tbsp. coconut oil
1 tsp. vanilla extract

DIRECTIONS

1. Combine all of the ingredients in a food processor.

2. Pulse until almond butter starts to form (about 3–4 minutes).

3. Once the almond butter is fully blended and creamy, store in a jar or other airtight container.

PUMPKIN SPICE SMOOTHIE

One of my favorite ways to have pumpkin is in this smoothie! It's thick and creamy and packed with good nutrition.

PREP TIME: 5 MIN. ● PALEO FRIENDLY, GLUTEN & DAIRY FREE

INGREDIENTS

Makes 1 serving
1 cup unsweetened almond milk
1 medium banana, frozen
¼ cup pumpkin puree
1 tbsp. creamy peanut butter or almond butter
1 tbsp. ground flax seeds
1 tsp. freshly grated ginger
2 tsp. pumpkin pie spice + extra for topping
Granola for topping (optional)

DIRECTIONS

1. Combine all of the ingredients in a blender and blend until smooth.

2. Top with extra pumpkin pie spice and granola, if desired. Enjoy!

PUMPKIN GREEN SMOOTHIE

Photograph by Megan Neveu

Pumpkin adds texture and more nutrition to this green smoothie that is healthy, delicious, and perfect any time of year!

PREP TIME: 5 MIN. • PALEO FRIENDLY, GLUTEN & DAIRY FREE

INGREDIENTS

Makes 1 serving
1 cup unsweetened
   almond milk
2 handfuls of spinach
¼ cup pumpkin puree
Juice from ½ lemon
1 tbsp. hemp seeds
2 tsp. freshly grated
   ginger
½ cup ice

DIRECTIONS

1. Combine all ingredients in a blender. Blend until smooth and enjoy!

PUMPKIN SPICE YOGURT BOWL

I like eating and cooking with siggi's® yogurt because it's higher in protein and lower in sugar, with simple ingredients like real pumpkin!

PREP TIME: 5 MIN. ● COOKING TIME: 5 MIN. ● GLUTEN FREE

INGREDIENTS

Makes 1 serving
½ cup siggi's® touch of honey whole-milk yogurt
⅓ cup pumpkin puree
¼ cup honeycrisp apple, diced
2 tsp. coconut oil
1 tsp. pumpkin pie spice
1 tbsp. pecans, chopped
1 tbsp. hemp seeds
2 tbsp. pumpkin seeds
1–2 tbsp. nut butter for drizzling on top

DIRECTIONS

1. Mix siggi's® yogurt and pumpkin puree together in a small bowl.

2. Over low heat sauté the apples with coconut oil and pumpkin spice just until they are softened.

3. Top yogurt bowl with apples, pecans, hemp seeds, and pumpkin seeds.

4. Drizzle nut butter on top and enjoy!

This recipe was created in partnership with siggi's®

siggi's ® pumpkin & spice is available as a seasonal flavor, often in the fall. You can enjoy this yogurt bowl any time of year by substituting it for the touch of honey whole-milk flavor.

PUMPKIN SPICE OVERNIGHT OATS

This oatmeal bowl practically makes itself in your fridge while you are sleeping! These overnight oats with pumpkin are thick and creamy and make for a great on-the-go breakfast option.

PREP TIME: 5 MIN. • RESTING TIME: 5 HOURS • DAIRY FREE

INGREDIENTS

Makes 1 serving
⅓ cup old-fashioned rolled oats
⅓ cup unsweetened almond milk
¼ cup pumpkin puree
1 tbsp. ground flax seeds
1 tbsp. hemp seeds
2 tsp. pumpkin pie spice
1 tsp. freshly ground ginger
Apple or banana slices, nuts, pumpkin seeds, and peanut or almond butter for topping

DIRECTIONS

1. Place the oats, almond milk, pumpkin puree, flax seeds, hemp seeds, pumpkin pie spice, and ginger in a bowl or a jar. Mix thoroughly to combine.

2. Cover and refrigerate overnight or for at least 5 hours.

3. In the morning, top with apple or banana slices, nuts, pumpkin seeds, and a drizzle of peanut or almond butter.

PUMPKIN APPLE BAKED OATMEAL

This breakfast bake embodies all of the flavors of fall—pumpkin, apples, cinnamon, ginger and pumpkin pie spice. I love a slice with almond butter on top for breakfast in the fall.

PREP TIME: 10 MIN. • COOKING TIME: 30–35 MIN. • DAIRY FREE

INGREDIENTS

Makes 8–10 servings
1½ cups old-fashioned oats
1 tbsp. ground flax seed
2 tsp. pumpkin pie spice
1 tsp. ground cinnamon
1 tsp. ground or fresh ginger
¼ tsp. ground nutmeg
1 tsp. baking powder
½ tsp. sea salt
½ cup pumpkin puree
1 large egg, lightly beaten
¼ cup pure maple syrup
¾ cup unsweetened almond milk
1 tsp. vanilla extract
⅓ cup diced apples + ½ apple thinly sliced for the top
2 tbsp. pumpkin seeds
Nut butter for topping

DIRECTIONS

1. Preheat oven to 350° F. Grease a 9-inch baking dish.

2. In a small bowl mix together the oats, flax seed, pumpkin pie spice, cinnamon, ginger, nutmeg, baking powder, and sea salt. Set aside.

3. In a large bowl, mix together the pumpkin puree, egg and maple syrup. Stir until combined. Add the almond milk and vanilla and stir until completely combined. Add in the diced apples and mix together one more time.

4. Add dry ingredients to the wet ingredients and stir until completely combined.

5. Pour batter into prepared baking dish. Slice the remaining apple into very thin slices and arrange on top of the oatmeal along with the pumpkin seeds.

6. Bake in the preheated oven for 30–35 minutes or until the top is set and slightly browned.

7. Remove from oven and let cool.

8. Slice, and enjoy with drizzled nut butter on top!

SAVORY PUMPKIN GINGER OAT BOWL

Explore the savory side of oatmeal with this pumpkin ginger oat bowl made with Quaker oats! It's a fun and delicious way to incorporate vegetables into your oatmeal, not to mention giving you protein and fiber to help fuel your morning. Oats are a good source of fiber and can help support a healthy digestive system.

COOKING TIME: 10 MIN. • DAIRY FREE

INGREDIENTS

Makes 1 serving
½ cup Quaker Old Fashioned Oats
¾ cup unsweetened almond milk
½ cup pumpkin puree
2 tsp. freshly grated ginger
Pinch of nutmeg
1½ tsp. pumpkin pie spice
1 cup spinach
1 egg

DIRECTIONS

1. In a small saucepan, heat oats with almond milk and pumpkin puree, stirring together until incorporated and oats begin to absorb the liquid.

2. Stir in ginger, nutmeg, and pumpkin pie spice, along with spinach, until spinach is incorporated

3. Remove from heat and transfer oats to bowl.

4. Cook egg sunny side up, until whites are set.

5. Top oat bowl with egg and enjoy!

Used with permission from The Quaker Oats Company

PUMPKIN CHIA SEED PUDDING

This pumpkin breakfast treat is packed with fiber and protein from the chia seeds. It gets extra thick in the fridge overnight and I love the spiced apples on top!

PREP TIME: 10 MIN. • RESTING TIME: 2 HOURS • GLUTEN FREE

INGREDIENTS

Makes 2 servings

For the chia seed pudding:

¼ cup chia seeds

½ cup low sugar vanilla yogurt

½ cup almond milk

2 tbsp. maple syrup

¼ cup pumpkin puree

1½ tsp. pumpkin pie spice

½ tsp. vanilla extract

For the apple topping:

¼ cup diced apples

1 tbsp. coconut oil

1–2 tsp. pumpkin pie spice + extra for topping

DIRECTIONS

1. Mix all the chia seed pudding ingredients together in a bowl until everything is well combined. Cover and place in the fridge to firm up for at least 2 hours or overnight.

2. Meanwhile, sauté the diced apples in the coconut oil and pumpkin pie spice.

3. Top the chia seed pudding with apples and an extra sprinkle of pumpkin pie spice when you're ready to eat!

PUMPKIN PANCAKES

Make any fall weekend feel extra special with a stack of these fluffy pumpkin pancakes. They are spiced to perfection with hints of nutmeg, ginger, and pumpkin pie spice. Top with maple syrup or creamy nut butter!

PREP TIME: 5 MIN. ● COOKING TIME: 10 MIN. ● GLUTEN & DAIRY FREE

INGREDIENTS

Makes 4–6 pancakes
1 cup LIBBY'S® 100% Pure Pumpkin
2 tbsp. coconut oil or butter, melted
2 eggs, lightly beaten
2 tbsp. maple syrup
1 tsp. vanilla extract
1¼ cups oat flour
½ tsp. baking soda
½ tsp. salt
1½ tsp. pumpkin pie spice
Fruit, maple syrup, or nut butter for topping

DIRECTIONS

1. In a small mixing bowl, stir together the pumpkin puree, coconut oil, eggs, maple syrup, and vanilla extract.

2. In a medium bowl, whisk together the oat flour, baking soda, salt, and pumpkin pie spice.

3. Mix the wet ingredients into the dry ingredients, until just combined. Don't over mix!

4. Heat a skillet with coconut oil or coconut oil spray. Use a ¼ cup measuring cup to scoop up the batter and pour into the pan.

5. Let cook until you start to see little bubbles forming around the edges, then flip. Repeat with remaining batter.

6. Top pancakes with fruit, maple syrup, or nut butter.

This recipe was created in partnership with Libby's

PUMPKIN CREPES

I've loved crepes ever since I had them while studying abroad in Paris. I know you'll love this pumpkin version as much as I do!

PREP TIME: 5 MIN. • RESTING TIME: 30 MIN. • COOKING TIME: 10 MIN.

INGREDIENTS

Makes 8-10 crepes
For the crepes:
2 large eggs
¼ cup butter, melted
¼ cup pumpkin purée
2 tbsp. sugar
¾ cup almond milk
½ tsp. vanilla extract
1 tsp. pumpkin pie spice
Sprinkle of nutmeg
Tiny dash of salt
8 tbsp. all-purpose flour
1 tbsp. coconut for
    greasing the pan

For the filling:
1 cup Greek yogurt
⅔ cup pumpkin puree
½ tsp. pumpkin pie spice
Bananas and hemp seed
    for topping
2 oz. dark chocolate
    melted for the drizzle
    on top

DIRECTIONS

1. Combine all of the crepe ingredients, except the flour, in a blender together. Then add in the flour, 1 tbsp. at a time, blending just until the flour has been mixed in. Chill the crepe batter for 30 minutes in the fridge.

2. Grease a crepe pan or nonstick pan with coconut oil and heat over medium heat. Pour about ¼ cup of batter into the pan and tip and tilt pan so that the batter spreads out really thin.

3. Cook each side of the crepe for 30 seconds before loosening up the edges with a spatula, and then flipping gently with help from the spatula. Repeat with remaining crepe batter.

4. In a medium-sized bowl combine the Greek yogurt, pumpkin puree, and pumpkin pie spice.

5. Spread thinly along the inside of the crepe. Fold in half and then fold one half over again to make triangles.

6. Top with sliced bananas, hemp seeds, and a drizzle of dark chocolate if desired!

PUMPKIN DUTCH BABY

Photograph by Megan Neveu

Perfect for an extra special weekend breakfast in the fall, this pumpkin Dutch baby is sure to be a favorite breakfast for years to come.

PREP TIME: 10 MIN. ● COOKING TIME: 20–22 MIN.

INGREDIENTS

Makes 1 10-inch skillet
4 tbsp. unsalted butter
3 large eggs at room temperature
⅔ cup 2% milk
¼ cup pumpkin puree
⅔ cup white whole-wheat flour
1 ¼ tsp. pumpkin pie spice
½ tsp. vanilla extract
¼ tsp. kosher salt
2 tbsp. coconut sugar or light brown sugar
Greek yogurt, maple syrup, pumpkin spice, and pumpkin seeds for topping

DIRECTIONS

1. Preheat oven to 425° F with cast-iron skillet inside. Allow skillet to heat in the oven for 15–20 minutes.

2. While the skillet is heating, bring any cold ingredients to room temperature.

3. Once the skillet is thoroughly heated, carefully remove from the oven and place butter in the skillet to melt.

4. While butter is melting, combine all remaining ingredients in a high-speed blender. Blend on medium-high for 30–45 seconds.

5. Immediately pour pancake batter into the skillet with the melted butter. Return to oven to bake for 15–18 minutes (pancake should be golden brown).

6. Turn oven off and leave in an additional 5 minutes.

7. Remove Dutch baby from the oven, top with toppings like Greek yogurt, maple syrup, pumpkin spice, and pumpkin seeds and enjoy!

PUMPKIN SHAKSHUKA

Photograph by Megan Neveu

Shakshuka is a traditional Mediterranean dish of poached eggs in a tomato sauce, with garlic and spices like cumin and paprika. This pumpkin version is a delicious savory brunch dish!

PREP TIME: 10 MIN. • COOKING TIME: 10–12 MIN. • GLUTEN FREE

INGREDIENTS

Makes 1 10-inch skillet
2 tbsp. olive oil
2 cloves garlic, minced
1 tsp. ground cumin
1 tsp. paprika
⅛ tsp. cayenne
½ tsp. ground ginger
1 can fire roasted
   tomatoes
1 cup pumpkin puree
1 tsp. salt
½ tsp. pepper
⅔ cup feta cheese,
   crumbled
4 eggs
Chopped cilantro, hot
   sauce, and lightly
   toasted pine nuts for
   topping

DIRECTIONS

1. Preheat oven to 375° F.

2. In a medium skillet, heat olive oil over medium heat, add minced garlic, and sauté until fragrant.

3. Stir in cumin, paprika, cayenne and ginger and then add tomatoes and pumpkin puree.

4. Simmer until mixture begins to thicken and season with salt and pepper.

5. Remove from heat and sprinkle crumbled feta on top of mixture.

6. Gently crack the eggs into the tomato pumpkin mixture, leaving a little space between each one.

7. Transfer skillet to the oven and bake until the eggs are just set, about 10–12 minutes.

8. Top with toasted pine nuts, cilantro, and hot sauce for a spicy kick!

BREADS, BITES & BARS

ONCE UPON A PUMPKIN BREAD

Photograph by Megan Neveu

This pumpkin bread is packed with the quintessential flavors of fall and will make your whole house smell delicious while it bakes.

PREP TIME: 10 MIN. • COOKING TIME: 50–55 MIN. • DAIRY FREE

INGREDIENTS

Makes 1 loaf
For the bread:
1 cup whole-wheat pastry flour
¾ cup oat flour
1 tsp. baking soda
2 tsp. pumpkin pie spice
1 tsp. cinnamon
¼ tsp. ground nutmeg
¼ tsp. cloves
½ tsp. salt
1½ cups pumpkin puree
¼ cup olive oil (one with a
   neutral flavor is best)
¼ cup unsweetened applesauce
2 eggs
¾ cup maple syrup
2 tbsp. pepitas

For the maple glaze:
½ cup powdered sugar
1 tbsp. pure maple syrup
1 tbsp. butter, melted
1 tbsp. unsweetened almond
   milk
1 tsp. pumpkin pie spice

DIRECTIONS

1. Preheat oven to 350° F and coat a 9x5-inch loaf pan with nonstick spray or coconut oil.

2. In a large bowl, whisk together the flours, baking soda, pumpkin pie spice, cinnamon, nutmeg, cloves, and salt.

3. In a separate large bowl, with a wooden spoon, mix together the pumpkin puree, olive oil, applesauce, eggs, and maple syrup.

4. Stir in the flour mixture and mix just until combined. Some lumps are okay.

5. Pour the batter into the greased pan and if desired, sprinkle pepitas on top.

6. Bake for 50–55 minutes, or until a toothpick inserted into the center comes out clean.

7. Meanwhile stir together all of the ingredients for the maple glaze in a small bowl.

8. Let the bread cool, remove from pan, and drizzle with maple glaze.

PUMPKIN CHOCOLATE CHIP BANANA BREAD

Pumpkin and banana were meant to be together in this bread, perfect for the fall! Just try resisting a warm slice right out of the oven!

PREP TIME: 10 MIN. • COOKING TIME: 50 MIN. • RESTING TIME: 10 MIN.

INGREDIENTS

Makes 1 loaf

1¼ cups mashed very ripe banana (about 3 bananas)

2 eggs

½ cup pumpkin puree

¼ cup coconut oil, melted

⅓ cup pure maple syrup

1 tsp. vanilla extract

2 cups whole-wheat pastry flour

2 tsp. pumpkin pie spice

1 tsp. baking soda

½ tsp. cinnamon

¼ tsp. salt

½ cup chocolate chips + more for sprinkling on top

DIRECTIONS

1. Preheat oven to 350° F. Grease the inside of a loaf pan.

2. Add mashed banana, eggs, pumpkin puree, coconut oil, maple syrup, and vanilla extract to a blender and blend until smooth and well combined. Pour into a large bowl.

3. Whisk all the dry ingredients, except the chocolate chips, together in a bowl and mix with the wet ingredients until just combined. Fold in the chocolate chips.

4. Pour batter into prepared pan. Sprinkle extra chocolate chips on top if desired.

5. Bake for 50 minutes. Allow bread to cool in the pan for 10 minutes, then remove and transfer to a wire rack to finish cooling.

PUMPKIN CARROT BREAD

Photograph by Megan Neveu

Wake up with a slice of this pumpkin carrot bread! I love the hearty texture and extra nutrition from the carrots and walnuts on top.

PREP TIME: 10 MIN. • COOKING TIME: 45 MIN. • DAIRY FREE

INGREDIENTS

Makes 1 loaf
½ cup old-fashioned oats
1 cup carrot, shredded
1½ cups whole-wheat flour
2 tsp. pumpkin pie spice
1 tsp. cinnamon
Pinch of nutmeg
Pinch of salt
1¼ tsp. baking soda
¾ cup pumpkin puree
¼ cup unsweetened
   applesauce
⅓ cup unsweetened
   almond milk
1 egg
½ cup pure maple syrup
2 tbsp. coconut oil, melted
1 tsp. vanilla extract
2 tbsp. pumpkin seeds
1–2 tbsp. walnuts,
   chopped (optional)

DIRECTIONS

1. Preheat the oven to 350° F and grease a loaf pan with coconut oil or cooking spray.

2. In a food processor, pulse oats until very fine. Grate carrots.

3. Combine flour, oats, pumpkin pie spice, cinnamon, nutmeg, salt, and baking soda in a large bowl. Whisk together until combined.

4. In a medium bowl, whisk together pumpkin puree, applesauce, almond milk, egg, maple syrup, coconut oil, and vanilla extract. Add wet ingredients, mix together until combined. Fold in grated carrots until just combined.

5. Pour batter into loaf pan and sprinkle pumpkin seeds and chopped walnuts on top if desired.

6. Bake for 45 minutes, or until a toothpick inserted into the middle comes out clean. Let cool completely and cut into pieces.

PUMPKIN ZUCCHINI BREAD

This is my favorite bread to make in early August when zucchini is in season and pumpkin season is just around the corner!

PREP TIME: 10 MIN. • COOKING TIME: 45–50 MIN. •
PALEO FRIENDLY, GLUTEN & DAIRY FREE

INGREDIENTS

Makes 1 loaf
2 cups blanched almond
    flour
2 tsp. baking powder
1 tsp. baking soda
2 tsp. pumpkin pie spice
½ tsp. cinnamon
¼ tsp. nutmeg
¼ tsp. sea salt
1 egg, lightly whisked
¼ cup maple syrup
¾ cup pumpkin puree
1 cup shredded zucchini,
    with excess moisture
    squeezed off using a
    paper towel
1 cup semisweet or
    dark chocolate chips
    (optional)

DIRECTIONS

1. Preheat oven to 350° F. Coat a 9x5-inch loaf pan with coconut oil or cooking spray.

2. In a large bowl, whisk together flour, baking powder, baking soda, pumpkin pie spice, cinnamon, nutmeg, and salt. Set aside.

3. In a separate bowl, whisk together egg, maple syrup, pumpkin puree, and zucchini until combined. Fold in chocolate chips if desired.

4. Pour the wet ingredients in with the dry ingredients, mixing until incorporated.

5. Pour pumpkin zucchini mixture into prepared loaf pan and bake for 45–50 minutes, or until a toothpick inserted in the center comes out clean.

PUMPKIN BLUEBERRY MUFFINS

Packed with fall flavors and made with nutritious ingredients, I love the combination of pumpkin and blueberries in these delicious and fluffy muffins!

PREP TIME: 10 MIN. • COOKING TIME: 20–22 MIN. • RESTING TIME: 10 MIN. •
PALEO FRIENDLY, GLUTEN & DAIRY FREE

INGREDIENTS

Makes 12 muffins
1 cup + 2 tbsp. gluten free oat flour
1 cup blanched almond flour
2 tsp. pumpkin pie spice
¼ tsp. salt
¾ tsp. baking soda
2 eggs, slightly beaten
⅓ cup pumpkin puree
⅓ cup pure maple syrup
1 tsp. vanilla extract
½ cup unsweetened almond milk
1 tbsp. coconut oil
1 tsp. fresh lemon juice
1 cup fresh or frozen blueberries

DIRECTIONS

1. Preheat oven to 350° F. Line 12 muffin cups with liners and spray the inside of the liners with nonstick cooking spray so they do not stick.

2. In a large bowl, whisk together 1 cup oat flour (reserving the 2 tbsp. for later), almond flour, pumpkin pie spice, salt, and baking soda.

3. In a separate large bowl, mix together eggs, pumpkin puree, maple syrup, vanilla, almond milk, coconut oil, and lemon juice until smooth and well combined. Add dry ingredients to wet ingredients and stir until just combined.

4. In a small bowl toss blueberries and remaining oat flour together, then gently fold them into the batter.

5. Divide batter evenly in each muffin tin. Bake for 20–22 minutes.

6. Transfer pan to a wire rack to cool for 10 minutes then remove muffins from pan and place on wire rack to cool completely.

A handful of blueberries is a good source of fiber and vitamin C. Add them to any of the oatmeal, yogurt bowl, or smoothie recipes in this book for a natural boost of sweetness and nutrients!

PUMPKIN PEANUT BUTTER CHOCOLATE CHIP MUFFINS

Photograph by Megan Neveu

There's truly nothing quite like a plump pumpkin muffin that is extra moist with hints of chocolate chips! If you're a peanut butter fan like me, you'll love this irresistible combination.

PREP TIME: 10 MIN. • COOKING TIME: 20–25 MIN. • GLUTEN & DAIRY FREE

INGREDIENTS

Makes 12 muffins
¾ cup pumpkin puree
½ cup shredded
   zucchini, squeeze out
   excess moisture with a
   paper towel
¾ cup natural creamy
   peanut butter
2 large eggs
¼ cup pure maple syrup
2 tsp. vanilla extract
½ tbsp. almond milk
1 cup oat flour
1 tsp. baking powder
2 tsp. pumpkin pie spice
¼ tsp. salt
⅓ cup semisweet or
   dark chocolate chips
   (optional)

DIRECTIONS

1. Preheat oven to 350° F. Line a 12-cup muffin tin with muffin liners and spray the inside with cooking spray to prevent muffins from sticking to liners.

2. In a large bowl, mix together pumpkin puree, zucchini, peanut butter, eggs, maple syrup, vanilla extract, and almond milk until smooth.

3. Stir in the oat flour, baking powder, pumpkin pie spice, and salt until smooth. Fold in the chocolate chips if desired.

4. Evenly divide batter into muffin liners.

5. Bake 20–25 minutes until toothpick comes out clean. Transfer muffins to wire rack to cool and enjoy.

FALL IN A BALL

These snack balls are the perfect healthy snack to have in the fall. They're loaded with protein, healthy fat, and fiber!

PREP TIME: 20 MIN. • PALEO FRIENDLY, GLUTEN & DAIRY FREE

INGREDIENTS

Makes 12 balls
2 pitted medjool dates
2½ tbsp. water
½ cup pumpkin puree
¼ cup raw cashews
2 tbsp. coconut oil, melted
½ cup blanched almond flour
1 tbsp. ground flax seed
1 tbsp. hemp seeds
2 tsp. chia seeds
2 tsp. pumpkin pie spice
1 tsp. freshly grated ginger
Pinch of sea salt
¼ cup pepitas

DIRECTIONS

1. Add dates and water to the bowl of a food processor and process a few times until dates begin to break down a bit and form a paste.

2. Next add in pumpkin puree, cashews, and coconut oil and pulse until well combined.

3. In a small bowl mix almond flour, flax seed, hemp seeds, chia seeds, pumpkin pie spice, ginger, and salt.

4. Scoop the wet ingredients out of the food processor and add to the dry ingredients and mix until well combined. Fold in the pepitas.

5. Once the ingredients are well combined, use a cookie scoop to portion and roll into balls.

6. Store in an airtight container in the fridge and enjoy!

PUMPKIN DONUTS WITH A MAPLE PUMPKIN SPICE GLAZE

Make baked donuts at home with this delicious Simple Mills Pumpkin Muffin & Bread Mix! I love that this mix is made with nutrient-dense ingredients and, like all of their products, nothing artificial ever.

PREP TIME: 5 MIN. • COOKING TIME: 25–30 MIN. • GLUTEN & DAIRY FREE

INGREDIENTS

Makes 6 donuts
For the muffins:
1 package Simple Mills Pumpkin Muffin & Bread Mix

For the pumpkin spice maple glaze:
½ cup powdered sugar
2 tbsp. maple syrup
Juice of ½ lemon
2 tsp. pumpkin pie spice + extra for topping

DIRECTIONS

1. Follow package instructions for muffins to make the batter.

2. Grease a donut pan with cooking spray and portion batter into the pan.

3. Bake according to package directions for muffins, and while they are in the oven combine the ingredients for the pumpkin spice maple glaze.

4. Drizzle over warm donuts and top with extra pumpkin pie spice!

This recipe was created in partnership with Simple Mills

PUMPKIN CHICKPEA BLONDIES

Photograph by Megan Neveu

You'll be shocked to know there are chickpeas in these bars! Dare I say they might be my favorite healthy pumpkin treat ever?!

PREP TIME: 5 MIN. ● COOKING TIME: 27 MIN. ● GLUTEN & DAIRY FREE

INGREDIENTS

Makes 9 bars

1 can (15 oz.) chickpeas, rinsed and drained
½ cup unsweetened, creamy peanut butter
⅓ cup pumpkin puree
⅓ cup pure maple syrup
2 tsp. vanilla extract
1 tsp. pumpkin pie spice
¼ tsp. baking powder
¼ tsp. baking soda
⅓ cup milk or dark chocolate chips + extra for sprinkling on top
Coarse sea salt, like Maldon, for sprinkling on top

DIRECTIONS

1. Preheat oven to 350° F and spray an 8x8-inch pan with cooking spray or coconut oil.

2. Combine all ingredients in a food processor except for the chocolate chips and sea salt. Pulse until batter is smooth.

3. Remove from food processor and fold in chocolate chips.

4. Pour batter into prepared baking pan and sprinkle extra chocolate chips on top if desired.

5. Bake for 27 minutes or until the center is set.

6. Let cool, sprinkle sea salt flakes on top, and cut a slice to enjoy!

PUMPKIN PIE SHORTBREAD BARS

Made with simple ingredients and layers of pumpkin goodness, you'll love these pumpkin pie bars as a fun fall treat!

PREP TIME: 10 MIN. • COOKING TIME: 40 MIN. •
PALEO FRIENDLY, GLUTEN & DAIRY FREE

INGREDIENTS

Makes 9 bars

For the shortbread crust:

2½ cups blanched almond flour
½ cup coconut oil
¼ cup maple syrup
1 tsp. vanilla extract
Couple pinches of salt

For the pumpkin pie filling:

2½ cups pumpkin puree
¼ cup maple syrup
⅓ cup full-fat coconut milk
1 egg
1 tsp. vanilla extract
1 tbsp. pumpkin pie spice
¼ tsp. salt

DIRECTIONS

1. Preheat oven to 350° F.

2. Mix together the ingredients for the shortbread crust together in a bowl.

3. Add the mixture to an 8x8-inch square baking pan with parchment paper and press it into the corners to make an even layer.

4. Combine the filling ingredients in a small bowl and pour the filling into the prepared crust and smooth over with a spatula or spoon.

5. Bake for 40 minutes in the middle of the oven, or until the filling is not jiggly. It will look exactly like pumpkin pie!

6. Let cool, cut, and top with whipped cream or coconut cream, and pecan pieces if desired.

COOKIES

PUMPKIN CHOCOLATE CHIP COOKIES

A classic cookie with a pumpkin spin on it! You can't go wrong with pumpkin and chocolate all in one healthy cookie!

PREP TIME: 10 MIN. ● COOKING TIME: 12 MIN. ●
PALEO FRIENDLY, GLUTEN & DAIRY FREE

INGREDIENTS

Makes 12 cookies
⅓ cup pumpkin puree
½ cup creamy almond butter
1 large egg
1 tsp. vanilla extract
⅔ cup coconut sugar
3 tbsp. coconut flour
½ cup finely ground almond flour
1 tsp. baking soda
½ cup dark chocolate chips
Sea salt for topping

DIRECTIONS

1. First, preheat oven to 350° F and spray a baking sheet with nonstick cooking spray. Set aside.

2. Next, place all ingredients except sea salt into a medium bowl and mix until combined.

3. Use a cookie scoop to portion out the cookie dough onto the baking sheet.

4. Bake for 12 minutes.

5. Transfer cookies from pan to a cooling rack and sprinkle on coarse sea salt for the final touch.

PUMPKIN COOKIE SKILLET

This pumpkin cookie skillet is the perfect treat for two or four, and something about eating it right out of the skillet makes it extra fun!

PREP TIME: 10 MIN. ● COOKING TIME: 20 MIN. ●
PALEO FRIENDLY, GLUTEN & DAIRY FREE

INGREDIENTS

Makes 1 10-inch skillet
1 cup blanched almond flour
2 tsp. pumpkin pie spice
¼ tsp. baking soda
⅓ cup LIBBY'S® 100% Pure
   Pumpkin
⅓ cup unsweetened
   almond butter
¼ cup maple syrup
1 egg
¼ cup coconut oil, melted
1 tsp. vanilla extract
1 tbsp. unsweetened
   almond milk
½ semisweet or dark
   chocolate chips + more
   for sprinkling on top
Sea salt, pumpkin seeds,
   and almond butter for
   topping (optional)

DIRECTIONS

1. Preheat the oven to 325° F. Grease a skillet pan or round cake pan with cooking spray.

2. In a medium bowl whisk all the dry ingredients, except for the sea salt.

3. In a separate bowl combine the pumpkin puree, almond butter, maple syrup, egg, coconut oil, vanilla extract, and almond milk.

4. Add the wet to the dry and stir until combined. Fold in chocolate chips and pour batter into skillet. Sprinkle a few more chocolate chips on top.

5. Bake for 20 minutes, remove from oven, and let cool. Sprinkle with sea salt and pumpkin seeds, and drizzle with almond butter if desired.

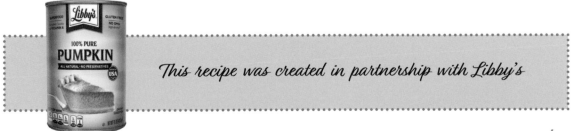

This recipe was created in partnership with Libby's

PUMPKIN SNICKERDOODLES

These snickerdoodles are a classic cookie that get even better with the addition of pumpkin and pumpkin spice!

PREP TIME: 10 MIN. • RESTING TIME: 30 MIN. • COOKING TIME: 12 MIN.

INGREDIENTS

Makes 18 cookies

For the cookie dough:

1½ cups all-purpose flour
2 tsp. pumpkin pie spice
½ tsp. cinnamon
½ tsp. baking soda
1 tsp. cream of tartar
½ tsp. salt
½ cup unsalted butter, softened
½ cup coconut sugar
¼ cup brown sugar
1 egg yolk
1 tsp. vanilla extract
¼ cup pumpkin puree

For the pumpkin spice sugar coating:

2 tbsp. coconut sugar
1 tsp. pumpkin pie spice

DIRECTIONS

1. Preheat the oven to 350° F and line a baking sheet with parchment paper or a silicone baking mat.

2. In a medium bowl combine flour, pumpkin pie spice, cinnamon, baking soda, cream of tartar, and salt. Set aside.

3. In a large mixing bowl, using an electric mixer, cream together the butter, coconut sugar, and brown sugar until well combined.

4. Mix in the egg yolk and vanilla extract, then mix in the pumpkin puree, stopping to scrape down the sides of the bowl as needed.

5. Add the dry ingredients to the wet ingredients and mix until just combined.

6. Refrigerate for 30 minutes.

7. Mix the pumpkin pie spice and sugar together in a small bowl

8. Remove the cookie dough from the fridge and portion out using a cookie scoop.

9. Roll each cookie in the pumpkin spice sugar mixture and place on a baking sheet.

10. Bake for about 12 minutes until the cookies are set. Let cool and enjoy!

PILLOWY PUMPKIN WHITE CHOCOLATE CHIP COOKIES

Pillowy pumpkin cookies are a must in the fall! They're fluffy and I love the combination of pumpkin and white chocolate chips.

PREP TIME: 10 MIN. ● RESTING TIME: 30 MIN. ● COOKING TIME: 11 MIN.

INGREDIENTS

Makes 18 cookies

¼ cup unsalted butter or coconut oil, melted
¾ cup brown sugar
1 tsp. vanilla extract
½ cup pumpkin puree
¼ cup unsweetened applesauce
¾ oat flour
¾ cup whole-wheat pastry flour
¼ tsp. salt
¼ tsp. baking powder
¼ tsp. baking soda
2 tsp. pumpkin pie spice
1½ tsp. cinnamon
Pinch of nutmeg
⅓ cup mini white chocolate chips

DIRECTIONS

1. In a medium bowl, combine melted butter and brown sugar until smooth.

2. Stir in the vanilla extract, pumpkin puree, and applesauce and set aside. In a large bowl, combine the flours, salt, baking powder, baking soda, pumpkin pie spice, cinnamon, and nutmeg.

3. Pour the wet ingredients into the dry ingredients and mix together with a spoon.

4. Fold in mini white chocolate chips. Cover the dough and refrigerate for 30 minutes.

5. Remove the dough from the refrigerator and preheat the oven to 350° F and line a baking sheet with parchment paper.

6. Use a cookie scoop to portion out the dough and bake for 11 minutes.

7. Repeat with remaining dough, let cool, and enjoy!

PUMPKIN COOKIES WITH CREAM CHEESE FROSTING

These pumpkin cookies with cream cheese frosting taste like fall, and I know you'll love them as much as I do!

PREP TIME: 15 MIN. • COOKING TIME: 12 MIN. • GLUTEN FREE

INGREDIENTS

Makes 18 cookies

For the cookie dough:
1½ cups almond flour
½ cup coconut flour
1½ tsp. pumpkin pie spice
½ tsp. baking soda
2 tsp. baking powder
¼ tsp. salt
1 egg
1 cup pumpkin puree
¼ cup maple syrup
1 tbsp. coconut oil, melted
2 tsp. vanilla extract

For the frosting:
4 tbsp. butter, softened
8 oz. cream cheese, softened
1 tsp. vanilla extract
½ cup powdered sugar
¼ tsp. pumpkin pie spice + extra for topping

DIRECTIONS

1. Preheat the oven to 375° F.

2. In a medium bowl whisk together almond and coconut flour plus pumpkin pie spice, baking soda, baking powder, and salt.

3. In another small bowl whisk the egg with the pumpkin puree, maple syrup, melted coconut oil, and vanilla extract.

4. Add the wet ingredients to the dry and mix until combined.

5. Use a cookie scoop to portion the dough onto a parchment lined baking sheet. Use your palm to gently press the cookie dough down.

6. Bake for approximately 12 minutes.

7. To make the frosting, place softened butter, cream cheese, and vanilla in a medium bowl. Beat until well combined. Add powdered sugar and pumpkin pie spice and continue to beat on high speed until fluffy.

8. Spread frosting on cooled cookies and sprinkle with additional pumpkin pie spice!

PUMPKIN OAT BREAKFAST COOKIES

These savory pumpkin oat breakfast cookies are something you'll want to wake up to all fall long. The chewy oats complement the taste of pumpkin and cranberry and finish with a pumpkin seed crunch! Oats have a relatively unique nutrition profile compared to other whole grains.

PREP TIME: 10 MIN. • RESTING TIME: 5 MIN. • COOKING TIME: 10 MIN. • DAIRY FREE

INGREDIENTS

Makes 18 cookies
1¼ cups Quaker Quick 1-Minute Gluten Free Oats
¼ cup hemp seeds
2 tbsp. dried cranberries
1 tbsp. chia seeds
2 tsp. baking powder
2 tsp. pumpkin pie spice
1 tsp. ginger
1 tsp. nutmeg
½ tsp. salt
¾ cup pumpkin puree
2 medium-sized eggs
½ cup unsweetened almond milk
1 tbsp. almond butter
3 tbsp. maple syrup
2 tsp. vanilla extract
¼ cup pumpkin seeds, unsalted

DIRECTIONS

1. Preheat oven to 350° F.

2. Spray a baking sheet lined with parchment paper with cooking spray.

3. In a medium bowl, whisk together oats, hemp seeds, cranberries, chia seeds, baking powder, pumpkin pie spice, ginger, nutmeg, and salt. Set aside.

4. In a separate medium-sized bowl, whisk pumpkin puree, eggs, almond milk, almond butter, maple syrup, and vanilla. Slowly stir into the dry ingredients.

5. Fold in pumpkin seeds, and let the batter sit for 5 minutes.

6. Use a cookie scoop or a tablespoon to drop dough two inches apart on the baking sheet. Bake for 10 minutes, then let cool completely on a cooling rack before serving.

Used with permission from The Quaker Oats Company

PUMPKIN SNOWBALL COOKIES

Like healthier donut holes, these snowball cookies with pumpkin puree and pumpkin pie spice will satisfy your craving for a pumpkin treat in a healthy way!

PREP TIME: 5 MIN. ● COOKING TIME: 22 MIN. ● GLUTEN & DAIRY FREE

INGREDIENTS

Makes 12 cookies
For the cookie dough:
1¼ cups almond flour
1 tbsp. coconut flour
⅓ cup coconut sugar
½ tbsp. pumpkin pie spice
1 tsp. cinnamon
¼ cup coconut oil
1 egg yolk, whisked
¼ cup pumpkin puree
2 tbsp. crushed walnut pieces (optional)

For the coating after baking:
2 tbsp. powdered sugar
1 tbsp. pumpkin pie spice + extra for topping

DIRECTIONS

1. Preheat oven to 300° F, and line a cookie sheet with parchment paper.

2. In a large mixing bowl combine almond flour, coconut flour, coconut sugar, pumpkin pie spice, and cinnamon. Mix together.

3. Add coconut oil, egg yolk, and pumpkin puree. Combine thoroughly and add in optional walnut pieces and stir in.

4. Roll tablespoon-size pieces of dough into balls and place on cookie sheet. Bake cookies in oven for 22 minutes.

5. While cookies are still warm, roll them in the powdered sugar and pumpkin pie spice. Sprinkle additional pumpkin pie spice on top and enjoy!

DIPS &
PASTAS

PUMPKIN TURMERIC HUMMUS

Photograph by Megan Neveu

Pumpkin puree adds texture and fall flavor to this classic hummus recipe. Taking the shells off of the chickpeas makes it extra creamy and delicious!

PREP TIME: 10 MIN. • GLUTEN & DAIRY FREE

INGREDIENTS

Makes 1½ cups hummus
2 cloves garlic
1 can chickpeas, drained, rinsed, and with shells removed
⅔ cup pumpkin puree
2 tbsp. tahini
1 lemon, juiced
½ tsp. turmeric
1 tsp. crushed red pepper flakes
½ tsp. salt
½ tsp. pepper
¼ cup extra-virgin olive oil + extra for drizzling on top
1 tbsp. pumpkin seeds, toasted, or pine nuts for topping

DIRECTIONS

1. Peel the garlic cloves and place in a food processor to mince.

2. Add the chickpeas, pumpkin, tahini, lemon juice, turmeric, red pepper flakes, salt, and pepper and pulse until combined.

3. Pour in the olive oil and continue pulsing until silky smooth.

4. Place in a small bowl and top with a drizzle of olive oil, toasted pumpkin seeds, or pine nuts.

PUMPKIN DESSERT HUMMUS

Perfect for dipping apple slices into, this pumpkin dessert hummus packs extra nutrition from the pumpkin puree and chickpeas and makes for the perfect snack!

PREP TIME: 10 MIN. • GLUTEN & DAIRY FREE

INGREDIENTS

Makes 1½ cups hummus
1 can chickpeas, drained and rinsed
½ cup creamy, unsweetened peanut butter
⅓ cup maple syrup
⅓ cup LIBBY'S® 100% Pure Pumpkin
1 tsp. vanilla extract
2 tsp. pumpkin pie spice
Pinch of salt
½ cup mini or regular dark chocolate chips

DIRECTIONS

1. Combine all of the ingredients except for the chocolate chips in the bowl of a food processor.

2. Pulse until smooth and blended.

3. Transfer to a bowl and fold in chocolate chips.

4. Serve with apple slices.

This recipe was created in partnership with Libby's

PUMPKIN CACIO E PEPE BOWTIES

Cacio e pepe literally translates to "cheese & pepper." For my take on this classic Italian dish, you know I had to add some pumpkin! It's a simple and delicious recipe you'll love long after pumpkin season is over!

PREP TIME: 10–12 MIN. • COOKING TIME: 10 MIN. • VEGETARIAN

INGREDIENTS

Makes 4 servings

1 box bowtie pasta
1 cup reserved pasta water
1 tsp. olive oil
4 tbsp. unsalted butter, divided
3 cloves garlic, minced
Pinch of salt
1 tsp. freshly cracked black pepper + extra for topping
⅔ cup pumpkin puree
Pinch of pumpkin pie spice
1 cup finely grated Parmesan cheese
¼ cup pecorino cheese, grated
Parmesan shavings for topping

DIRECTIONS

1. Prepare pasta according to package directions. Once the pasta has cooked, reserve 1 cup of the water.

2. While the pasta is cooking, heat a large skillet and add the oil and 2 tbsp. of butter. Once the butter melts, stir in the garlic with a pinch of salt and 1 tsp. pepper. Toast for 1–2 minutes.

3. Stir in the pumpkin puree until combined.

4. Stir in 1 cup of the reserved pasta water. Stir in the remaining 2 tbsp. of butter and the pumpkin pie spice and bring the mixture to a simmer.

5. Add in the pasta and toss it together. Reduce the heat to low and stir in the Parmesan and pecorino.

6. Toss until the cheese is melted and becomes somewhat of a sauce with the water and the pasta.

7. If needed, you can add in more water to thin out the sauce.

8. Serve with extra Parmesan shavings and freshly cracked black pepper.

PUMPKIN RAVIOLI WITH CRISPY SAGE AND TOASTED PINE NUTS

This recipe is like fall in a bowl—it's the perfect cozy meal for a chilly fall night. Each bite will remind you of your favorite things about the season! LIBBY'S® 100% Pure Pumpkin fills every ravioli with the taste of pumpkin we all know and love.

PREP TIME: 25 MIN. ● RESTING TIME: 30 MIN. ●
COOKING TIME: 5 MIN. ● VEGETARIAN

INGREDIENTS

Makes 2 dozen ravioli
For the ravioli dough:
3 eggs
Pinch of salt and pepper
1 cup all-purpose flour

For the filling:
1 cup LIBBY'S® 100% Pure Pumpkin
½ cup part-skim ricotta cheese
½ tsp. cayenne pepper
1 tbsp. butter, melted
½ tsp. salt
Pinch of nutmeg
1 tsp. red pepper flakes

DIRECTIONS

For the ravioli:

1. In a food processor, add eggs, salt, and pepper and pulse.

2. Add half of flour, pulse, and add the rest. Continue to pulse until dough comes together (about 1 minute). If dough is overly sticky, continue to add more flour, 1 tablespoon at a time, until texture softens.

3. Remove dough and roll into two equal balls. Cover and refrigerate dough for 30 minutes.

4. Remove dough from fridge. Using a pasta roller, feed dough through roller until it is a paper-thin consistency. Note: Depending on the pasta roller this will take multiple rolls through the tool.

5. Lay sheet of thin dough flat on a flat surface. Place ½ tbsp. of filling onto dough. Repeat until you have a row of filling on the dough about 3 inches apart from each other.

(Continued)

For the assembly:
1 tbsp. butter
¼ cup pine nuts
¼ cup pumpkin seeds
1 cup cooked butternut
   squash, cubed
8 sage leaves
¼ cup shredded
   Parmesan cheese for
   topping

6. Using a ravioli stamper, stamp around each pocket of filling. Repeat with remaining dough.

7. Bring a pot of lightly salted water to a vigorous boil. Slowly add the ravioli and let cook for about 4 minutes.

8. Using a slotted spoon, remove the ravioli and place on a plate not on top of each other.

For the filling:

1. Combine pumpkin, ricotta, cayenne pepper, melted butter, salt, nutmeg, and red pepper flakes in a small bowl.

To assemble:

1. In a medium skillet over medium-low heat, melt the butter and add the pine nuts and pumpkin seeds. Add butternut squash and sage. Stir together gently.

2. Add 3–4 ravioli at a time. Mix them around the pan so that they are gently coated in the different flavors.

3. Plate and top with Parmesan cheese.

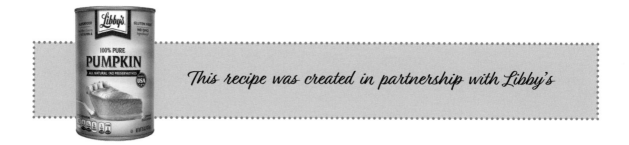

This recipe was created in partnership with Libby's

PUMPKIN MAC AND "CHEESE"

Warm up on a chilly fall night with this creamy, dairy-free pumpkin mac and "cheese"! Made with LIBBY'S® 100% Pure Pumpkin, the sauce is full of flavor and extra nutrition.

PREP TIME: 10–12 MIN. • COOKING TIME: 10 MIN. • DAIRY FREE, VEGETARIAN

INGREDIENTS

Makes 4 servings
1 box of the pasta of your choice
1½ cups LIBBY'S® 100% Pure Pumpkin
½ cup frozen butternut squash, thawed in the microwave
½ cup vegetable broth
2 tbsp. nutritional yeast
2 tsp. olive oil
1 clove garlic
1 tsp. red pepper flakes
Pinch of salt and pepper

DIRECTIONS

1. Cook pasta according to package directions.

2. In a blender, combine all of the other ingredients until smooth.

3. Transfer sauce to a small saucepan and heat over medium low.

4. Combine with cooked pasta of your choice. Add spinach or other vegetables too!

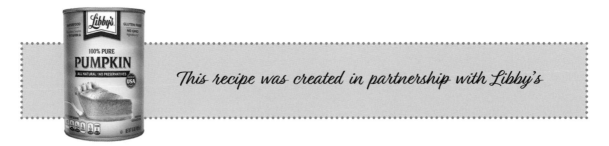

This recipe was created in partnership with Libby's

SOUPS & CHILIS

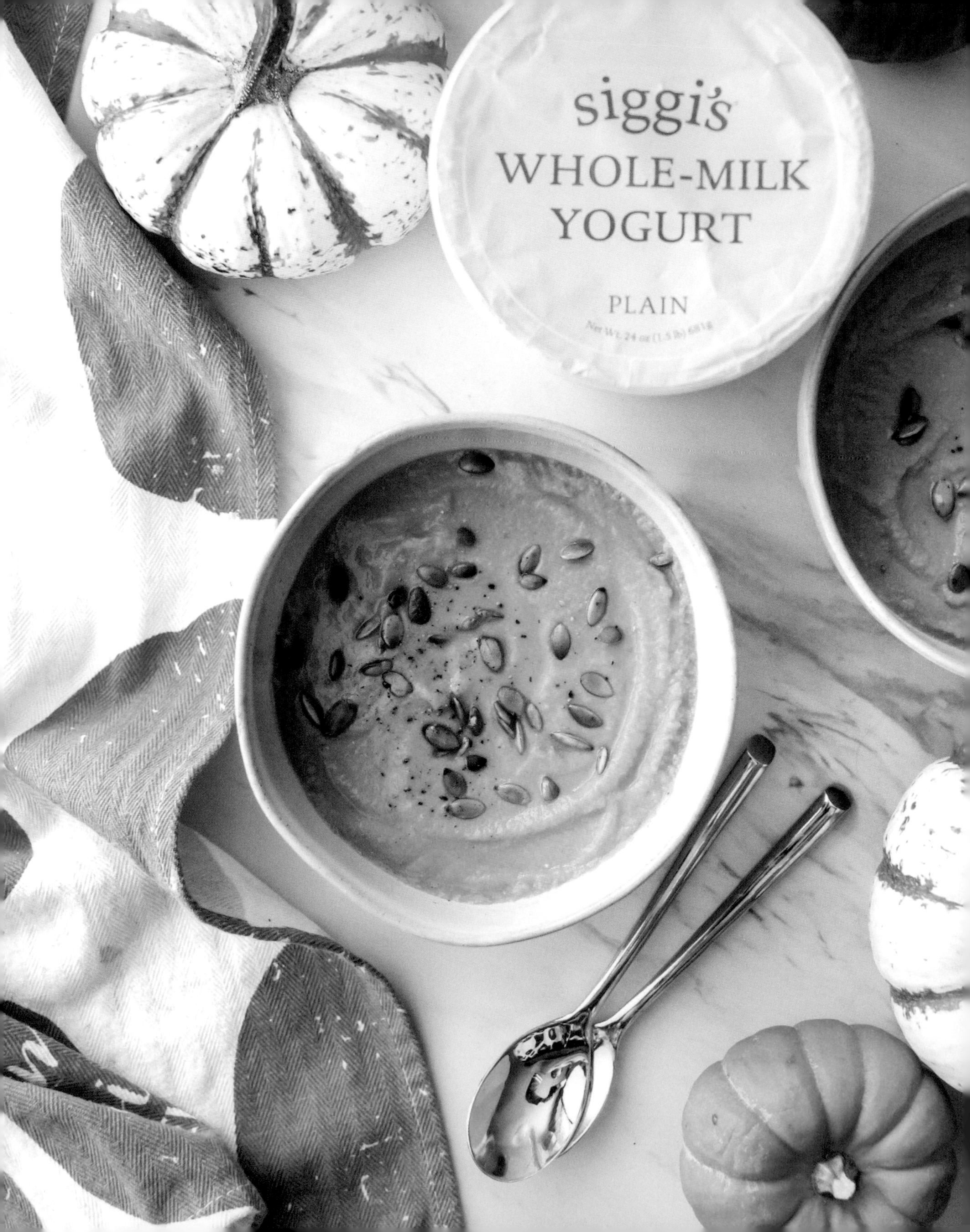
siggi's
WHOLE-MILK
YOGURT
PLAIN

LEMON PUMPKIN SOUP

This simple, yet satisfying savory pumpkin soup is easy to make and is sure to warm you up in chillier weather. The siggi's® yogurt gives it its thick, creamy texture and is made with simple ingredients and not a lot of sugar.

PREP TIME: 10 MIN. • COOKING TIME: 25 MIN. • GLUTEN FREE, VEGETARIAN

INGREDIENTS

Makes 4 servings
1 tbsp. olive oil
1 shallot, diced
2 cloves garlic, minced
2½ cups low sodium
   vegetable broth
2 cups pumpkin puree
1 cup siggi's 4% whole-
   milk yogurt
¼ cup freshly squeezed
   lemon juice
1½ tsp. freshly grated
   ginger
1 tsp. red pepper flakes
1 tsp. turmeric
Pinch of nutmeg
Salt & freshly ground
   pepper to taste + extra
   pepper for topping
¼ cup pumpkin seeds,
   toasted

DIRECTIONS

1. In a soup pot over medium heat, add the olive oil, shallot, and garlic. Cook for 2–3 minutes, or until translucent and fragrant.

2. Add the remaining ingredients, except the pumpkin seeds, stir to combine, and bring to a light simmer for 10 minutes.

3. Transfer soup mixture to a blender and blend together or use an emulsion blender to puree the soup.

4. Pour soup back into pot and continue simmering for an additional 10 minutes.

5. Meanwhile, over low heat, toast the pumpkin seeds on a pan. It will just take a couple of seconds for the seeds to lightly toast, so don't step away to prevent them from burning!

6. Portion soup into bowls and top with toasted pumpkin seeds and freshly ground black pepper.

This recipe was created in partnership with siggi's®

PUMPKIN GINGER BISQUE

Pumpkin ginger bisque is everything you want and more from a fall soup. It's extra creamy and will warm you up from the inside out.

PREP TIME: 10 MIN. ● COOKING TIME: 25 MIN. ● GLUTEN FREE, VEGETARIAN

INGREDIENTS

Makes 4 servings
2 tbsp. olive oil
3 cloves garlic, minced
1 shallot, diced
3 cups vegetable broth
1 can pumpkin puree
1½ cups cubed butternut squash (frozen works great, just make sure you heat it up according to the package directions before adding to the soup)
1 lemon, juiced
2 tsp. fresh ginger
1 tsp. cinnamon
½ tsp. ground turmeric
½ tsp. red pepper flakes
½ tsp. salt
1 tsp. freshly grated pepper + extra for topping
½ cup freshly grated Parmesan cheese + extra for topping
Toasted pumpkin seeds for topping (optional)

DIRECTIONS

1. In a large pot heat olive oil and add the garlic and shallot. Stir until fragrant.

2. Add vegetable broth, pumpkin puree, and the cubed butternut squash and mix until combined.

3. Add lemon, ginger, cinnamon, turmeric, red pepper flakes, and salt and pepper.

4. Blend soup using an immersion blender or transfer (1 cup at a time) to a high-speed blender (like a Vitamix) to achieve the creamy blended texture.

5. If blending in a blender, add back into the soup pot and let simmer for about 5 more minutes.

6. Grate the Parmesan cheese into the soup pot and add extra pepper if desired.

7. Add to a bowl and garnish with extra cheese or toasted pumpkin seeds!

PUMPKIN CAULIFLOWER CURRY

Filled with plant-based protein and lots of veggies, you'll love how delicious and easy to make this curry with pumpkin is!

PREP TIME: 10 MIN. ● COOKING TIME: 25–30 MIN. ●
GLUTEN & DAIRY FREE, VEGETARIAN

INGREDIENTS

Makes 4 servings
1½ tbsp. coconut oil
1 medium shallot, minced
1½ tbsp. minced fresh
   ginger
1½ tbsp. minced garlic
2 bell peppers, sliced
3 tbsp. red Thai curry
   paste
1 can pumpkin puree
1 can chickpeas
1 can light coconut milk
2 tbsp. maple syrup or
   coconut sugar
1 tsp. ground turmeric
Salt and pepper to taste
1 tbsp. coconut aminos
1½ cups cauliflower, riced
Rice or quinoa for serving
¼ cup cashews, and
   cilantro for topping
   (optional)

DIRECTIONS

1. Heat a large pot over medium heat. Add coconut oil, shallot, ginger, and garlic.

2. Sauté for 2–3 minutes, stirring frequently.

3. Add peppers and curry paste and stir. Cook for 2 minutes more

4. Then add pumpkin puree, chickpeas, coconut milk, maple syrup, turmeric, salt, pepper, and coconut aminos. Stir together. Bring to a simmer over medium heat. Then add the riced cauliflower. Reduce heat to low, and cover.

5. Cook for 10–15 more minutes, stirring occasionally. Serve as is or over rice or quinoa.

6. Top with cashews and cilantro if desired.

VEGGIE PUMPKIN OAT CHILI

This plant-based spin on chili made with Quaker oats is packed with veggies and the goodness of oats! Oats are a relatively powerful super grain and possess more possibilities than you may have thought.

PREP TIME: 10 MIN. • COOKING TIME: 10 MIN. • DAIRY FREE, VEGETARIAN

INGREDIENTS

Makes 4 servings
2 tbsp. extra virgin olive oil
1 shallot, diced
2 cloves garlic, minced
2¼ cups vegetable broth
1 15-oz. can pumpkin puree
1 can crushed, fire roasted tomatoes
1 can black beans
½ cup frozen butternut squash
2 tbsp. chili powder
½ tsp. ginger
1 tbsp. crushed red pepper flakes
1 tbsp. dried oregano
1 cup Quaker Steel Cut Oats
Salt and pepper to taste
Fresh cilantro, pumpkin seeds, or jalapeño for topping

DIRECTIONS

1. Heat the olive oil in a large soup pot over medium-high heat. Add the shallot and garlic and cook until just tender and fragrant.

2. Add the vegetable broth, pumpkin puree, tomatoes, black beans, butternut squash, chili powder, ginger, crushed red pepper, and oregano.

3. Stir and bring to a simmer. Then reduce heat and add oats. Cook for about 4–5 minutes until oats are incorporated.

4. Season to taste with salt and pepper and top with fresh cilantro, pumpkin seeds, or jalapeño for a spicy kick.

Used with permission from The Quaker Oats Company

PUMPKIN TURKEY CHILI

Pumpkin adds texture and nutrition to this chili that is packed with flavor (and extra veggies)! My favorite way to eat it is with sliced avocado on top.

PREP TIME: 15 MIN. ● COOKING TIME: 25–30 MIN. ●
PALEO FRIENDLY, GLUTEN & DAIRY FREE

INGREDIENTS

Makes 4 servings
2 tbsp. olive oil
1 medium yellow onion, diced
2 medium bell pepper (red, yellow, or orange), diced
4 cloves garlic, minced
1⅓ lbs. ground turkey or chicken (90 to 93% lean)
1 can pumpkin puree
1 28-oz. can diced fire roasted tomatoes, with liquid
¼ cup tomato paste, no salt added
1 cup reduced-sodium chicken or vegetable broth
2 tbsp. chili powder
1 tbsp. cocoa powder
1 tbsp. pumpkin pie spice
2½ tsp. ground cumin
1 tsp. kosher salt
½ tsp. ground black pepper
½ tsp. cayenne pepper (optional)
Avocado, arugula, yogurt, pumpkin seeds, tortilla chips, or cheese for topping

DIRECTIONS

1. Coat a large pot with olive oil over medium-high heat.

2. Add the onion and bell pepper and sauté, stirring occasionally, until the onion softens.

3. Add the garlic, stir everything together, and cook until fragrant, about 30 seconds.

4. Add the ground turkey and use a spatula to break up the meat as it cooks. Continue to cook about 6–7 minutes, until fully cooked.

5. Add pumpkin puree, diced tomatoes, tomato paste, broth, chili powder, cocoa powder, pumpkin pie spice, cumin, kosher salt, black pepper, and cayenne pepper (if desired). Stir together. Reduce heat and simmer for 20–30 minutes, stirring occasionally.

6. Transfer to a bowl and top with toppings such as avocado, arugula, a dollop of yogurt, pumpkin seeds, tortilla chips, or cheese!

PUMPKIN PIES & CAKES

PUMPKIN SPICE LATTE PIE

Photograph by Megan Neveu

Inspired by the flavors of a pumpkin spice latte, this pie is smooth and creamy like our favorite fall drink!

PREP TIME: 10 MIN. • COOKING TIME: 10 MIN. + 40–50 MIN.

INGREDIENTS

Makes 1 pie

For the crust:

1 package pumpkin granola

2 tbsp. butter or coconut oil, melted

For the filling:

1 can pumpkin puree

½ cup packed brown sugar

¼ cup granulated sugar

½ cup mascarpone cheese

2 tsp. pumpkin pie spice + extra for topping

4 eggs, lightly beaten

6 tbsp. brewed espresso

Whipped cream and caramel sauce for topping (optional)

DIRECTIONS

1. To make the crust, pre-heat the oven to 325° F, and place entire package of granola in a food processor. Pulse until granola resembles graham cracker crumbs.

2. Pour into a small bowl and add butter or coconut oil. Mix until incorporated.

3. Pour granola mixture into a pie pan and use your fingers to pack it into the bottom and up the sides.

4. Bake for 10 minutes.

5. To make the filling, in a large bowl combine pumpkin, sugars, mascarpone cheese, and pumpkin pie spice.

6. Stir in eggs and espresso until combined. Pour pumpkin mixture into piecrust.

7. Bake 45–50 minutes until the center is set. Let cool and chill.

8. Top slices with whipped cream, caramel sauce, and extra pumpkin pie spice!

CLASSIC HEALTHY PUMPKIN PIE

Photograph by Megan Neveu

This classic pumpkin pie is perfect for your holiday table. It's easy to make with just a few simple ingredients. I used LIBBY'S® 100% Pure Pumpkin, which always reminds me of good times in the kitchen baking with my mom.

PREP TIME: 10 MIN. • COOKING TIME: 50–55 MIN. • RESTING TIME: 1 HOUR • DAIRY FREE (OPTIONAL)

INGREDIENTS

Makes 1 pie
1 store-bought pie crust
1 can LIBBY'S® 100% Pure Pumpkin
3 eggs
¼ cup maple syrup
¼ cup coconut sugar
¼ cup milk of your choice
1 tsp. vanilla extract
1½ tsp. pumpkin pie spice
½ tsp. nutmeg
½ tsp. ground ginger
½ tsp. allspice
¼ tsp. salt
Whipped cream and pecans for topping

DIRECTIONS

1. Unwrap the pie crust and place into a pie dish.

2. In a large bowl, mix together the pumpkin puree, eggs, maple syrup, coconut sugar, milk, vanilla, pumpkin pie spice, nutmeg, ground ginger, allspice, and salt. Mix until completely smooth. Pour into pie pan.

3. Cover the edges of the pie with a pie shield or foil. Bake for 50–55 minutes. The middle of the pie should be set.

4. Let cool, and place in the fridge for at least an hour before serving. Top slices with whipped cream and pecans.

This recipe was created in partnership with Libby's

NAKED PUMPKIN CAKE

Photograph by Megan Neveu

Celebrate the season with this beautiful and delicious cake recipe perfect for any autumn occasion! Made with Simple Mills Pumpkin Bread & Muffin Mix, it's delicious and made with nutrient-dense ingredients.

PREP TIME: 20 MIN. • COOKING TIME: 30 MIN. • GLUTEN & DAIRY FREE

INGREDIENTS

Makes 1 cake
2 packages Simple Mills Pumpkin Bread & Muffin Mix
2 containers Simple Mills Vanilla Frosting

Optional tools:
1–2 6x2-inch round cake pans
Cake leveler
Angled icing spatula

DIRECTIONS

1. Prepare pumpkin muffin and bread mix according to instructions for bread. Pour batter into a greased 6x2-inch round cake pan and bake according to package directions.

2. Remove from oven and let cool on a baking rack.

3. Once both cakes have cooled, cut them in half horizontally so you have two equal cake halves.

4. Place one layer of the pumpkin cake onto a plate or cake stand. Use an angled icing spatula to scoop out about ¼ cup of vanilla frosting on top of cake.

5. Use the spatula to spread the icing around the top of the cake and lightly spread it on the sides so that you can still see the cake through the thin layer of frosting.

6. Place the next layer on top and begin icing the same way. Repeat with remaining layers of cake.

7. Decorate the cake with garnishes like leaves or use a small pumpkin as a topper.

This recipe was created in partnership with Simple Mills

MINI PUMPKIN BUNDT CAKES

Shaped like a pumpkin and spiced just right, these mini pumpkin Bundt cakes made with Simple Mills Pumpkin Muffin & Bread Mix are festive and flavorful, and I love that the mix is made with real pumpkin!

PREP TIME: 5 MIN. • COOKING TIME: 25–30 MIN. • GLUTEN & DAIRY FREE

INGREDIENTS

Makes 4 mini Bundt cakes
For the cakes:
1 package Simple Mills Pumpkin Muffin and Bread Mix
2 cinnamon sticks
Pumpkin pie spice for sprinkling on top

For frosting:
½ cup powdered sugar
2 tbsp. maple syrup
Juice of ½ lemon

DIRECTIONS

1. Prepare batter according to package directions for muffins.

2. Divide evenly into greased mini Bundt pans.

3. While the cakes are cooking, combine the ingredients for the frosting.

4. Let the Bundts cool. Gently cut the bottom off of the cakes and place two together, forming the pumpkin shape. Place a cinnamon stick through the middle to resemble a pumpkin stem.

5. Drizzle with frosting and sprinkle with extra pumpkin pie spice!

This recipe was created in partnership with Simple Mills

PUMPKIN ROLL

This pumpkin roll makes a statement on your table. It's perfect for the holidays or whenever you feel like baking something special with your family!

PREP TIME: 15 MIN. ● COOKING TIME: 10 MIN. ● RESTING TIME: 1 HOUR

INGREDIENTS

Makes 1 roll
For the cake:
3 eggs
½ cup sugar
⅔ cup LIBBY'S® 100% Pure Pumpkin
¾ cup all-purpose flour
2 tsp. cinnamon
1 tsp. pumpkin pie spice + extra for sprinkling on top (optional)
1 tsp. nutmeg
1 tsp. baking soda

For the cream cheese filling:
½ cup butter, softened
1 package (8 oz.) cream cheese, softened
½ cup confectioners' sugar + extra for sprinkling on top (optional)
1 tsp. vanilla extract
Juice of ½ lemon

DIRECTIONS

1. Preheat the oven to 350° F and line an 11x15-inch baking sheet with parchment paper. Spray the parchment paper with cooking spray.

2. Using a handheld or stand mixer, beat eggs with sugar and pumpkin puree.

3. Combine the dry ingredients in a separate bowl and whisk until combined.

4. Add the dry ingredients to the wet and mix together until just combined. Spread the batter onto the parchment-lined baking sheet. Use a spatula to spread it so that it's even and not higher in some spots.

5. Bake for 10 minutes, then remove from oven. (You want the cake to be moist and flexible so that it will easily roll.)

6. Invert the cake on to a cheese cloth or thin dish towel (big enough for the entirety of the cake). Peel off the parchment paper and gently roll the cake up with the towel. Let cool completely for at least 1 hour (can be placed in the fridge).

(Continued)

7. While the cake is cooling beat the butter and cream cheese together with a handheld or stand mixer. Add the rest of the ingredients and beat until combined and creamy.

8. Once the cake has cooled completely, remove from the fridge and let warm up on the counter for a few minutes.

9. Gently unroll the cake from the towel and spread frosting evenly on top, leaving about a 1-inch border across the top of the cake. Gently and slowly roll the cake up again, this time without the towel. If some of the frosting pops out, that is okay!

10. Slice into pieces and top with additional pumpkin pie spice or confectioners' sugar if desired!

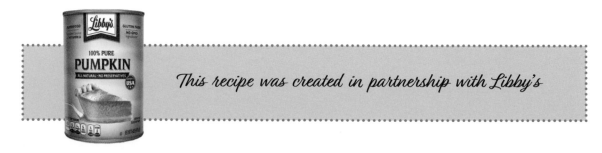

This recipe was created in partnership with Libby's

PUMPKIN CHEESECAKE

I make this recipe every year for my family for Thanksgiving dessert, and I hope you enjoy it just as much as we do. To me it symbolizes thankfulness and gratitude for the love, laughter, and beautiful moments from the past year. Enjoying it with the people around you is truly the biggest blessing of all!

PREP TIME: 20 MIN. ● COOKING TIME: 1 HOUR ● RESTING TIME: 1 HOUR

INGREDIENTS

Makes 1 cheesecake
1 cup graham cracker crumbs
2 tbsp. butter, melted
3 packages cream cheese, softened
¾ cup sugar
2 tsp. vanilla extract
¼ cup dark rum
4 eggs, room temperature
1 cup LIBBY'S® 100% Pure Pumpkin
1½ tsp. pumpkin pie spice
½ tsp. salt
Fresh berries and whipped cream for topping

DIRECTIONS

1. Preheat oven to 325° F.

2. Combine graham cracker crumbs with melted butter. Mix until combined.

3. Press onto the bottom and slightly up the side of 9-inch springform pan. Bake for 10 minutes and let cool completely.

4. Meanwhile, in the bowl of a mixer add the softened cream cheese and sugar. Beat on medium-high speed until just combined (not over beating the batter is key for cheesecake!).

5. Add the vanilla and rum, and then room temperature eggs one at a time until just combined. After the final egg is incorporated into the batter, stop mixing.

(Continued)

6. Scoop out 2 cups of batter and place in a medium mixing bowl. Using a wooden spoon, stir in the pumpkin, pumpkin pie spice, and salt until combined. Begin adding big spoonfuls of each batter, the plain and the pumpkin, on top of the crust until you have used all of it.

7. Use a knife to gently swirl the batters together.

8. Bake for 1 hour. Turn oven off and let cool in oven for another hour. Once cooled, refrigerate for several hours or overnight.

9. Top with fresh berries and whipped cream and enjoy!

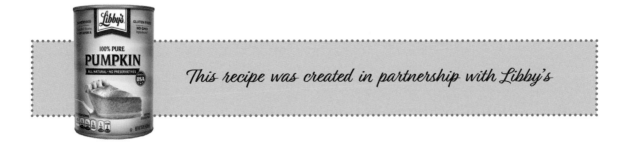

This recipe was created in partnership with Libby's

PUMPKIN SEEDS

EVERYTHING BUT THE BAGEL PUMPKIN SEEDS

Don't toss those pumpkin seeds! Roast them up for a good snack that is full of plant-based protein, fiber, and magnesium.

PREP TIME: 10 MIN. • COOKING TIME: 20 MIN. •
PALEO FRIENDLY, GLUTEN & DAIRY FREE

INGREDIENTS

Makes 1 cup

1 cup pumpkin seeds, rinsed

1 tbsp. olive oil

2 tbsp. Everything but the Bagel seasoning

DIRECTIONS

1. Preheat oven to 325° F.

2. Pat the pumpkin seeds dry with a paper towel, then toss in a bowl with olive oil and Everything but the Bagel seasoning.

3. Roast for about 20 minutes, tossing halfway through.

FOR YOUR FURRY FRIEND

PUMPKIN PEANUT BUTTER DOG TREATS

Pumpkin is a superfood for dogs! It's great for their digestion and can even help with an upset stomach. My dog's name is Pumpkin too, and true to his name he loves these treats!

PREP TIME: 10 MIN. • COOKING TIME: 18 MIN. • GLUTEN & DAIRY FREE

INGREDIENTS

Makes 24 treats
1 cup oat flour
½ cup creamy unsweetened peanut butter
⅓ cup pumpkin puree
1 tsp. cinnamon
¼ cup + 2 tbsp. low sodium chicken stock

DIRECTIONS

1. Preheat oven to 350° F. Spray a dog treat pan with cooking spray to prevent treats from sticking.

2. Combine oat flour, peanut butter, pumpkin puree, and cinnamon in a medium mixing bowl. Add stock and stir until well-combined. The dough will be thick.

3. Scoop about 1 tbsp. of dough into each mold of the dog treat pan or roll into a ball. Repeat with remaining dough.

4. Bake for 18 minutes, remove from oven, and let cool. For maximum freshness, store these in an airtight container or in the fridge.

I give my small dog half of one treat at a time!

ACKNOWLEDGMENTS

Mom and dad, I wouldn't be where I am without either of you. It's because of your hard work and sacrifices that am I a registered dietitian today and I will never take that for granted. Thank you for your selfless love and for everything you've done for me!

Lucy and Dorothy, growing up with you two as role models was what pushed me to strive for more and dream bigger—because I saw my big sisters do it! Thank you for always supporting my goals and cheering me on. There's nobody I look up more to than you two.

Rob, thanks for eating all of my pumpkin creations, hunting for pumpkin things with me, and dreaming my dreams with me. And most of all understanding that our kitchen will always be a mess, but a happy one. I am so lucky to have you in my life!

INDEX